Nettle Nook

A Year In The Life Of An Allotment

CHARLOTTE MANN

Piccalilli Publishing

NETTLE NOOK

Nettle Nook

A Year In The Life Of An Allotment

* * *

Words & Doodles

By

Charlotte Mann

For John & Alexander

* * *

Creating memories together that grow and will last beyond a lifetime...

Contents

Text Insert   iv
dedication   v

And So It Began...   1

The Tale Of Nettle Nook.   3

SPRING

Daffodils & Tulips   7

Frog Family   9

Hooray Woodlouse   11

False Widow   13

A Gentle Leek   15

Swifts   17

The Green Man   19

SUMMER

The Humble Spud   23

Badger Bandits   25

Grasshopper Dance   27

Sweetest Of Peas   29

Friendly Butterfly	31
Fuzzy Bee Hum	33
Scarecrow	35

AUTUMN

Wonkiest Of Carrots	39
Nettles	41
Gentleman Magpie	43
Mamma Mouse	45
Dreaming Spores	47
Guiding Fox	49

WINTER

Give A Hog A Hand	53
Caw Caw Crow	55
Mischievous Squirrel	57
The Sprout Babies	59
Robin Redbreast	61
Little Snowdrop	63
Pigeon Pie	65
Muddy Boots	67
Little Pink Shed	69
... And So	70
Photographs Of Nettle Nook	73

About The Author 92

Copyright © 2022 by Charlotte Mann

All rights reserved. No part of this book may be reproduced in any manner whatsoever without written permission except in the case of brief quotations embodied in critical articles and reviews.

First Printing, 2022

And So It Began...

The Tale Of Nettle Nook.

"This is the tale of Nettle Nook,
"Take some time to have a look,

Whether sun or rain or ice and snow,
This is a story of how things grow,

A suburban patch of countryside,
Planting and growing with eyes open wide,

It's really fulfilling and good for the soul,
A feeling of joy and making one whole."

Spring

"Fresh air in the morning, blue skies above, there's life all around, so show it some love..."

Daffodils & Tulips

"From frozen earth, comes the spring rebirth,

The buds and the flowers are beginning to show,

Where as roots and shoots are starting to grow,

But the splendour of a springtime bloom,

Fills the air with a sweet perfume,

When tulips and daffodils are a joy to the eye,

Winter is behind us, we've said goodbye."

Frog Family

"We are most grateful that you took your time,

Finding our pond to frolic and climb,

We hope to see some froglets soon,

Laying your eggs by the light of the moon,

We wish you well, that your spawn shall grow,

That our pond keeps them safe with its gentle flow,

For a family of frogs we'd welcome you,

To reside with us the whole year through."

Hooray Woodlouse

"Amongst the beetroot in rich dark soil,

You wriggle and wiggle above the turmoil,

A rake or trowel never does any harm,

Your grey little bodies have an armoured charm,

You clean all the veg plots of decay and debris,

We should really do more to appreciate thee..."

False Widow

"Solitary and silent upon her silken thread,

Wrapping and winding so she shall be fed,

Perhaps I've walked into her lair,

I really don't mind... as I really do care!

Eight legs and eyes I should not fear,

So instead when I see her I quietly cheer!

To share my greenhouse just isn't a chore,

So I smile at her each time, when I close the door."

A Gentle Leek

"Standing tall and green and part unseen,

Is a gentle leek.

A subtle flavour and one to savour,

Is a gentle leek.

A gardeners friend, and chefs godsend,

Is a gentle leek.

Soups or stews, whatever you choose,

Just use a gentle leek.

Swifts

"You fly so high a screech in the sky,

Life on the wing till you nest here in Spring,

Your faithful mate with a patient wait,

Till your chicks all hatch as there's good food to catch,

Then back on the wing till autumn you sing,

When you leave once again soaring high as a plane!

Then Africa you reach, over the veldt you shall screech."

The Green Man

"The Green man steadfast throughout the year,

Bringing us joy and seasonal cheer,

Overseeing my lush green plot,

A verdant thriving beauty spot!

For flora as told in old folklore,

From highest plant to lowly spore."

Summer

"The rays shine down, the warmth of the sun, time to be happy, the hard work's been done..."

The Humble Spud

"You can mash them and chip them boil and bake them too,

Cook them whole or slice them up just heat the whole way through,

Add butter, cheese or beans they all top well,

But roasting in an oven gives a gorgeous smell,

A sprinkle of herbs and a drizzle of oil,

Pop them on an open fire and wrap them in foil,

They say that you are humble but you are so versatile,

When tattie season's upon us it's really time to smile."

Badger Bandits

"With snuffling noses and long sharp claws,

The crunching of sweetcorn with their strong hard jaws,

Digging up potatoes and pumpkins in the patch,

Stopping in the moonlight for a good hard scratch,

Their determination is something to admire -

...Even though it's we which grow the food they desire."

Grasshopper Dance

"Sitting on a rhubarb leaf making clicking sounds,

Hopping and bobbing and jumping all around,

Forwards and backwards, left and to the right,

Tiny little grasshoppers just sit tight..."

Sweetest Of Peas

"You look so fragile when you gently climb,

Twisting and turning against the twine,

Blossoming purples, pinks and blues,

A myriad of beautiful pastel hues,

Curly and climbing, ever so high,

Reaching towards the summers sky."

Friendly Butterfly

"Fly up high butterfly fly!

Let your pretty wings lift you to the sky!

I know you like my leafy greens...

The kale, the cabbage and even the beans!

But if you take a deeper look,

There's flowers here at Nettle Nook,

You could feed, rest and pollinate,

As a butterfly garden could be really great!"

Fuzzy Bee Hum

"That sound in summer, you hear over and over,

A song of love to the red and white clover,

It zurrrs all around you, a sound you can trust,

When colours are plenty, and sweet scent is a must,

They have furry striped bodies, they're quick on the wing,

But there's naught to be scared of, they don't want to sting,

So during that time which commences in June,

Savour that song, it's a buzzing bee tune!"

Scarecrow

"With arms outstretched, stood firm in ground,

Your duty's to scare the birds around,

You've a head full of straw,

And a carrot for a nose,

Standing sentinel in the same old pose,

Keep the crops safe the whole year through,

Till I harvest the nook, and start anew."

Autumn

"Colours of ombré, orange and gold, a time for renewal, a sight to behold!"

Wonkiest Of Carrots

"You'd think a carrot would be easy to grow,

With its strong coloured flesh and steady flow,

Against all odds in deep clay soils,

It splits and twists and even coils,

Misshapen and ugly? That it may be,

But judging by taste, it's a wonderful tea!"

Nettles

"You're plentiful here upon my plot, but that's okay as I've picked a good spot,

You may be seen as only a weed, but I'm glad you've grown and gone to seed,

As I use you for teas and making good soaps,

You soothe my dry skin and fulfil all my hopes,

That I find you here, and you continue grow,

My medicinal friend, you help me to glow!"

Gentleman Magpie

"Watching from his treetop perch,

The magpie swoops from his branch of birch,

He spots the seeds, just laying bare,

To harvest his hunger in cool autumn air,

He strides out with a sense of pride,

A distinguished gent with eyes twinkling wide,

With a stretch of wings he embarks upon high,

Against the orange of an October sky,

His family calls as he sets down to roost,

A feast for his offspring, it's a welcome boost!"

Mamma Mouse

"Oh little mouse I see you,

Rushing about with so much to do,

So stop and sample a fruity delight,

A treat so big, your eyes twinkle bright!

There's enough for us all, so take some to share,

With your family and babies so fragile and bare,

Scurry them back to your safe little nest,

Eat on up little mouse, take a well deserved rest."

Dreaming Spores

"Producing spores, during downpours,

Carried on the breeze and floating by trees,

Nestled below, in earth that they grow,

Damp and shaded, the mushrooms have invaded!"

Guiding Fox

"Curled up on the grass in fresh morning air,

The sun shining down in a bright heatless glare,

By day you rest, your vigour to keep,

But when dusk time falls, a mate you shall seek,

A distinctive call, a screech, that we hear,

But it's only you, and so nothing to fear,

For centuries on you've guided us through,

The seasons of change, and a cold morning dew."

Winter

" To catch a snowflake, to wrap up warm, time to recharge, a chance to transform..."

Give A Hog A Hand

"I'm overjoyed to have noticed you, preparing to hibernate all winter through,

These colder seasons that lay the green bare, now food is scarcer you're getting quite rare,

For once a hog was a regular sight, but now it's time to heed their plight,

We need to act, lend a caring hand, so you'll survive little hedgehog across this land!"

Caw Caw Crow

" Winter crows a-cawing, stop and stand in awe,

Listen to their birdcall when night begins to fall,

They talk to one another and keep the roost secure,

The winter crows a-cawing are standing proud and sure."

Mischievous Squirrel

"Mischievous squirrel that I see, chasing and bounding from fence to tree,

Swinging onto the feeder to tip up the seeds, into the soil and over the swedes,

Here! I have kept a peanut or two, that I put aside just for you,

Scurry and bury them into the ground, somewhere safe, yet can still be found;

There's plenty of nuts stored here for you, to see you fed all winter through."

The Sprout Babies

"I planted you as tiny shoots but now you've got much deeper roots, you have shrugged off the April frost, it could have been at greater cost,

The pigeons came to give you a try, but you're safe under netting, so off they fly!

You survived the attack of the munching snails; it made you strong and hard as nails!

I created little copper rings, to keep you safe from all slimy things,

But last of all and not the least, they saw you as a broody feast...

You triumphed in the butterfly bout and all because you're the mighty sprout!

Now it's Christmas and you're on my plate, which always was a sprouts true fate!"

Robin Redbreast

"I hear you sing each morning perched upon the tree,

Please don't stop your birdsong as it really heartens me,

You stand your ground in winter, you chirp into the Spring,

Little Robin Redbreast, you're a delight upon the wing!"

Little Snowdrop

"With your long green shoots, you are a welcome sight; a perfect flower, a bell of white,

The first of the florals at the start of the year, giving us hope that Spring is near,

Pushing your way through the frost and the snow, and a hardened ground that cannot stop you grow,

Little snowdrop you're the star of the day - we know the warmth of the sun is now on its way!"

Pigeon Pie

"You hear the call for pigeon pie! an angered tone in the wind going by,

The realisation the crops have been had, you shake your head and brand them bad,

But who can blame them, if you really think - a tender shoot and a droplet drink,

Keeps them healthy and is mighty tasty; a gardener's reaction can be a tad hasty,

For pigeons you remain all year round,
keeping me company on frosted ground,

So a couple of shoots that go awry, is not just cause for pigeon pie!"

Muddy Boots

"Muddy boots, muddy boots, I'd be lost without you,

You're better than a welly or a nice new shoe.

You keep my ankles sturdy and my feet all secure,

Muddy boots, muddy boots, my comfort you ensure."

Little Pink Shed

"Little pink shed you put me in good stead, to tackle all the weeds ahead, you house all my tools, my pots and cans, so I can fulfil all my seasonal plans."

... And So

"You've read this little book, a year in the life
of Nettle Nook,

It's a place for calm with a gentle breeze, or the howl
of the wind amongst the trees...

For whichever season happens to fall, there will
always be stories that we'll surely recall!"

Photographs Of Nettle Nook

1. Apple Blossoms
2. Red Mason Bee
3. Cherry Blossom
4. Daffodil
5. Raindrops On Sprout Leaves
6. Basket Of Goodness
7. Green Man
8. Apple Tree
9. Fuzzy Bee Hum
10. Common Frog
11. Barley Corn
12. Artichoke
13. Passion Flower
14. French Lavender
15. Pink Beans
16. River Daisy
17. Slate Sign - made and designed by: Andreas Attic

 Charlotte resides in Greater Manchester, with her partner, two sons and cats. She has a keen interest in the natural world and artistic expression, so this particular project has been a welcome opportunity to combine the two.

www.ingramcontent.com/pod-product-compliance
Lightning Source LLC
Chambersburg PA
CBHW041508010526
44118CB00006B/187